250 Years of
HOLD MY ROOT BEER

The Commemorative Guide to the
World's Longest Group Project (1776-2026)

PHASE 01 of 03

By Backyard Logic

Technical Note on Production: This volume was developed using a "Human-in-the-Loop" methodology. While AI-assisted tools were utilized for schematic rendering and data synthesis, all content has been curated, architected, and extensively edited by human hands. The resulting arrangement, brand identity, and creative commentary are the proprietary intellectual property of the publisher.

Published by Backyard Logic
U.S.A.

First Edition: May 2026
Series: The Backyard Logic 250 Years Trilogy | Phase 01

ISBN: 979-8-9960744-0-2

Disclaimer: This book is intended for entertainment purposes only. While it contains historical facts, it is a work of humor. The author is not responsible for any sudden urges to buy a smoker, wear white sneakers, or start a revolution.

Semiquincentennial
(1776-2026)

- Phase One: The Revolutionary Startup
- Phase Two: The Expansion
- Field Manual of Unsolicited Advice
- Phase Three: The Modern Marvels
- Tactical Party Ops

Introduction: The 250-Year Pulse

You ever sit back and just think about the fact that we've been a country for 250 years, man? That's a long time to keep anything going. I knew a guy back home, "Shifty" Shelby, who couldn't keep a hamster alive for a long weekend, and here we are, managing an entire continent without a manual. That's that "Group Project" power, you know?

Being American is a specific kind of spirit. It's like we're all part of this giant, loud family reunion that's been happening since 1776, and nobody's quite sure who brought the potato salad, but we're all gonna eat it anyway. We are a nation built on "Hold my root beer and watch this."

Think about those original guys—the Founders. They were just out there in the woods, wearing wool in the middle of a swamp, riding on bird feathers, telling the biggest empire in the world, "Hey, we're good. We're going to start our own thing over here. It's going to have more snacks and way less royalty." That's a bold move, man. That's that "first day at a new school" energy, but with muskets.

And 250 years later, we're still doing it. We're still out here trying to figure out how to park a minivan and why the Wi-Fi acts up when it rains, but we're doing it together. We've got guys in Maine eating lobster rolls and guys in Arizona living in a literal oven, and somehow we all agree that a 44-ounce soda is a "medium."

This book isn't about the stuff you had to memorize in the 11th grade just to pass the test. It's about the vibe. It's about the crack in the bell, the three cent land deals, and the fact that we went to the moon just to see if we could hit a golf ball where there's no wind.

We're 250 years deep into the greatest "See What Happens" experiment in history. So, pull up a lawn chair, grab a cold one, and let's look at the receipts. Because if we've made it this far without accidentally deleting the whole thing, we're doing something right.

Welcome to the semiquincentennial anniversary, man.
It's been a wild ride.

PHASE ONE:
THE REVOLUTIONARY STARTUP

1776 - 1800s

Beta-testing a democracy.
No manual, high stakes, total flex.

John Hancock signed his name so large on the Declaration—some say because he wanted King George to be able to read it without his glasses. It was the 18th-century version of writing in ALL CAPS to make sure the point landed.

The Formal Break-up

The Declaration of Independence was basically the world's most formal break-up text. "It's not me, King George, it's definitely you. I'm keeping the dog and the colonies. Also, don't call me." It's the original "delete-your-number" energy.

The first U.S. Mint was established in 1792. Before that, Americans used Spanish coins, English pounds, and occasionally just traded tobacco leaves. We've been "figuring it out as we go" since day one.

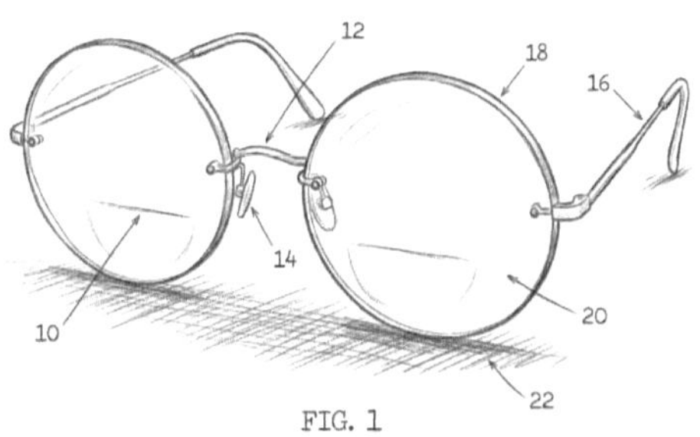

FIG. 1

Pioneer of the Side Hustle

Ben Franklin was basically the guy who posts "rise and grind" content while actually living on three hours of sleep and French wine. He's closing international deals in Paris at midnight, then waking up to invent bifocals just so he can see his own greatness. He's the original remote worker, crushing a side hustle before the rest of us even invented gourmet coffee.

In 1776, there was no "official" flag. People just sewed whatever they wanted. Some had 13 stripes, some had circles, some had a snake that said "Don't Tread on Me." It was the "Wild West" of graphic design.

FIG. 1

The National Bird Debate

We chose the Bald Eagle as our symbol because it looks majestic in photos. Ben Franklin wanted a turkey. Imagine a 50-yard-line flyover with a giant turkey. The National Anthem would feel a lot more like a Thanksgiving invitation.

The White House didn't get indoor plumbing until 1833.
For the first 33 years, the Leader of the Free World had to
walk to an outhouse in the middle of a D.C. winter.
That'll keep you humble real quick.

The Woolen Uprising

We celebrate 1776 like it was a grand gala. In reality, it was 56 guys in wool suits, in Philadelphia, in July, with no AC. The Declaration wasn't just a political statement; it was a desperate plea to finish the meeting so they could go stand near a block of ice.

July 4th wasn't the day we won the war; it was just the day we sent the letter. The war actually lasted another seven years. We just really liked the date for the party.

From Parchment to "U Up?"

Founding a nation with a feather and a jar of black goo is a wild level of commitment. You couldn't just backspace or drop a "my bad" emoji when the ink smeared. Today, we treat history like a group chat. If Jefferson had a phone, the Declaration would've just been a spicy X thread and a middle-finger emoji sent to King George.

In 1776, there were about 2.5 million people in the colonies. Today, there are more people than that living in just the city of Chicago. We've gone from a "small startup" to a global conglomerate.

Liberty on Credit

Paul Revere started the Revolution on a borrowed horse he never returned—essentially a high-stakes payday loan. He galloped into history on someone else's equity. Today, we honor that legacy by charging our lattes to credit cards we'll pay off "later." Turns out, American freedom was founded on debt.

We bought 828,000 square miles in the Louisiana Purchase for $15 million. That's about 3 cents an acre. Today, that won't even buy you a "Large" fountain drink at a gas station.

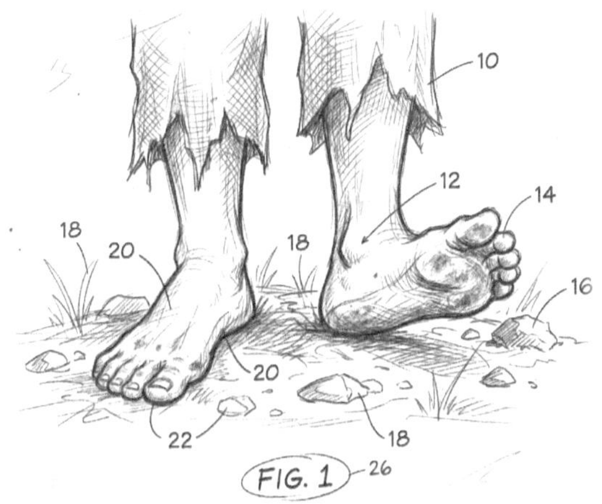

The Three-Cent Rebellion

We fought the world's biggest navy over breakfast taxes with zero shoes. It's the ultimate "why though?" move. Like a Gen Zer questioning a pointless task, we just didn't vibe with the authority. I'm not paying that three cents.

On the 50th anniversary of the country (1826), both Thomas Jefferson and John Adams died on the exact same day—July 4th. It's like they checked the calendar and said, "Okay, the 50-year warranty is up. My work here is done."

Wigs and Wild Vibes

Man, we think these guys were fossils, but Monroe was eighteen, and Hamilton was 21. Just some kids with a dream and a forehead full of destiny. It was basically a bunch of teenagers with great hats just acting out because the vibes were off.

We dumped 342 chests of tea into Boston Harbor. That's roughly 18.5 million cups. We didn't just protest; we gave the entire Atlantic coastline a caffeine addiction.

The Big Steep

What is the deal with the tea? We're so upset about the price that we dump it in the ocean? Now nobody has tea! It's the ultimate "Hold my Root Beer" move. We turned the Atlantic into a giant, salty teapot. Who's drinking that? No one's drinking that!

The U.S. Constitution is only 4,500 words long. That's shorter than the Terms and Conditions for a basic iPhone update. We built a superpower on less text than it takes to play Candy Crush.

Pioneers vs. Buffering

Listen, back in '76, moving from Philly to New York was a whole mission. You had smallpox, mud, and your horse might just die on you. Now, we're on a train, heated seats, complaining the Wi-Fi is slow. Man, we really lost the plot. How are we the same species?

In the early 1800s, a letter from D.C. to the Kentucky frontier took weeks to arrive. Americans essentially lived in total freedom because the government was too slow to find them. It was a golden era of liberty—mostly because of bad roads.

Interior Design Under Fire

In 1814, the British burned Washington, apparently forgetting they'd already lost the first round. While they were playing with matches, Dolley Madison was saving George's portrait. It's a masterclass in unwavering resolve: the house is literally on fire, but we aren't leaving without the good art. We're in it to win, even if the wallpaper's melting.

PHASE TWO: THE EXPANSION

(Walking West & Worrying Later)

1800s - 1900s

We wired the world, lit the night, and conquered gravity.

LIBERTY FACT

The Oregon Trail was 2,170 miles long. Over 400,000 pioneers walked it. A lot of them didn't walk because they wanted to explore; they walked because they owed money back East. That's that "fresh start" power, man.

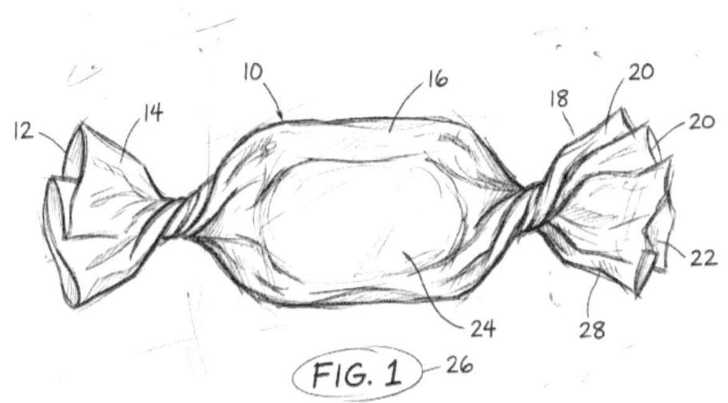

Taffy: The Final Frontier

The Atlantic was fine, but we got bored. We wandered West—no snacks, just fighting grizzlies and everyone in our way—to see if that water was "bluer." We hit the coast, realized we ran out of planet, and went, "Well, now what? Build a pier and sell salt-flavored sugar?" Manifest Destiny: a 3,000-mile walk for a cavity.

LIBERTY FACT

In the mid-1800s, the "Balloon Frame" revolutionized housing, replacing heavy timber with light, standardized lumber. Suddenly, homes were easy to build and even easier to order from a catalog. It was the ultimate expression of liberty: the freedom to live in a house that arrived on a train like a giant Lego set.

The Ultimate Property Flip

In 1825, Governor DeWitt Clinton looked at his perfectly fine Great Lakes property and decided it needed an ocean view. He dug a 363-mile ditch all the way to the Atlantic, turning quiet lakefront into a global commercial hub. It's the ultimate American "renovation"—completing a massive engineering miracle just to upgrade your zip code and property value.

LIBERTY FACT

In 1858, Cyrus Field laid the first undersea telegraph cable, connecting America and Europe. For the first time, news crossed the Atlantic in minutes rather than weeks. It was a massive leap for global liberty—finally, we could receive bad news from across the ocean in real-time.

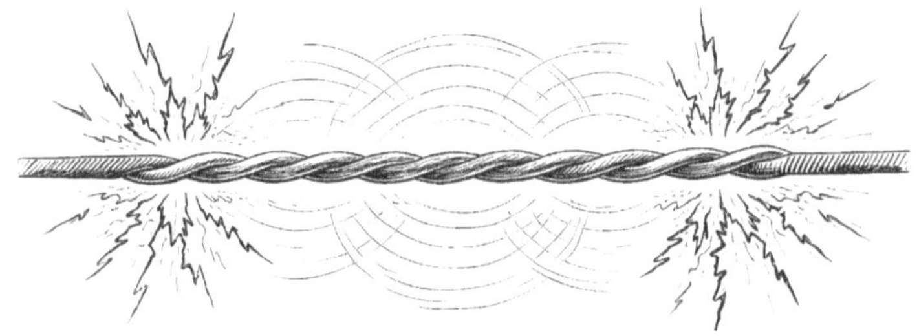

The OG Ghosting

In 1844, Samuel Morse tapped out "What hath God wrought," the first official telegraph message, unknowingly inventing the ability to be mad at someone from forty miles away. We traded face-to-face shouting matches for the glorious safety of distance. It was the birth of the indirect burn, paving the way for "per my last email" and 180 years of dodging awkward confrontations.

LIBERTY FACT

The California Gold Rush started at Sutter's Mill in 1848. In 1849, over 90,000 "Forty-Niners" arrived. They found roughly $2 billion in gold. Most of them spent all that gold on $12 eggs and shovels. It's always the guy selling the shovels who wins.

Panning for Likes

The 1848 Gold Rush was the ultimate viral hustle.
Thousands sprinted West because the FOMO was real!
We haven't changed; we just traded freezing riverbeds
for the "Inside Scoop" social media trends. We're still just
pioneers chasing the dream!

LIBERTY FACT

The Liberty Bell cracked on its very first use in 1752. It was re-cast, but it cracked again in 1846 during George Washington's birthday celebration. We haven't tried to ring it since. Smart. Why risk a third strike?

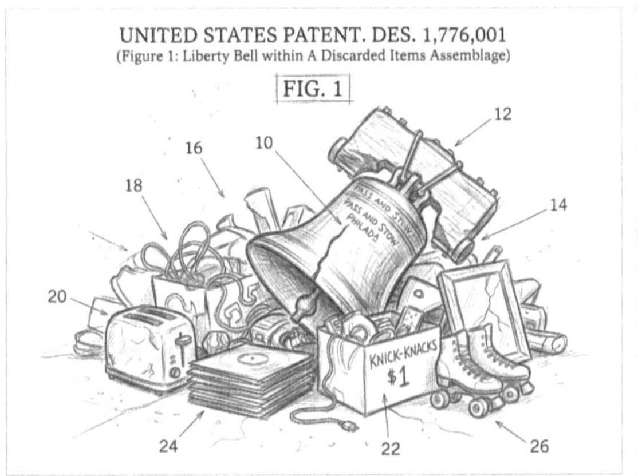

The Ultimate Yard Sale Comeback

We got this "Liberty Bell" from England, rang it once,
and it split wide open. Usually, you see something
cracked in the alley, you keep walking. But we were like,
"Nah, man, that's still good! Just lean it against the wall."
We turned a defective return into a national treasure.
It's not garbage; it's "vintage" liberty.

LIBERTY FACT

In 1851, Jacob Fussell established the first commercial ice cream factory, transforming an elite delicacy into an affordable American staple. By industrializing production, he democratized the dessert, ensuring frozen treats were no longer reserved solely for the wealthy. It was a victory for liberty, finally granting every citizen the unalienable right to a massive brain freeze.

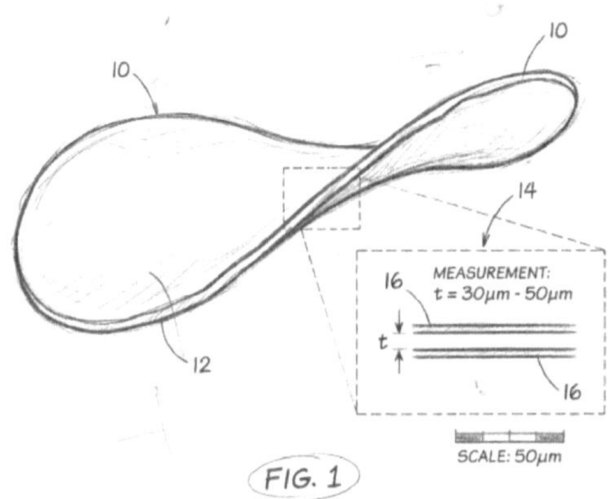

FIG. 1

Crum's Crispy Revenge

George Crum had a customer who kept sending his fried potatoes back for being too thick. George finally snapped, sliced them paper-thin out of pure spite, and accidentally invented the potato chip. That's the American dream right there. We'll redo a mistake until it's perfect, then realize we can probably get five bucks a bag for it.

LIBERTYFACT

During the Civil War, the Union army consumed massive amounts of "hardtack," a tooth-shattering flour biscuit. It was so incredibly durable, legend has it that soldiers often used the leftovers as makeshift building materials. It's the only war won on a diet of literal bricks.

The Suplex of the Union

Before he led the gang, Abe was out there as a licensed bartender and a champion wrestler with only one recorded loss in 300 matches. He was just a lanky boy with big dreams, unknowingly training to suplex a divided nation back together in '61. It's that pure American vibe—always keeping that big stick ready.

LIBERTY FACT

The Pony Express only lasted 19 months (1860–1861). It was a financial disaster, but it became a legend. It's the original tech bubble that burst, just with more cowboy hats and actual dust.

Sprinting vs. Snacking

The Pony Express hired teenagers to sprint horses across the wilderness. It went bust because horses eventually realize they're doing all the work, and the teens just wanted to lay in the dirt. Turns out, "a lot of very tired, very dusty kids" is a tough way to keep a business open.

LIBERTY FACT

The First Transcontinental Railroad was joined with a Golden Spike at Promontory Summit, Utah, on May 10, 1869. The news was sent instantly via telegraph. It was the first "national live stream" in history. The telegraph just read: "DONE."

GPS: Guessing Proves Sufficient

We decided to build a railroad from both sides of the country at the same time and just hope we met in the middle. Imagine that logistics meeting. "You start in Sacramento, I'll start in Omaha, and we'll meet at that weird-looking rock in Utah." They didn't have GPS; they just had a "Can-Do" attitude and a lot of dynamite.

LIBERTY FACT

Yellowstone National Park was established by Congress in 1872. It was the first national park in the world. We looked at a volcano that wants to erase the continent and thought, "Let's keep that as a landmark." That's that "High Risk, High Reward" thinking.

Sticking Nature in a Box

We stared at Yellowstone—a place where the ground literally boils and explodes—and said, "This is beautiful. Let's make sure nobody ever builds a CVS here." We protected it so people can drive four thousand miles to sit in their car and stare at a bison through the sunroof.

The world's first "skyscraper" was the Home Insurance Building in Chicago, built in 1885. It was only 10 stories tall. Today, there are suburban Target stores bigger than that. But at the time, people thought it was touching the atmosphere.

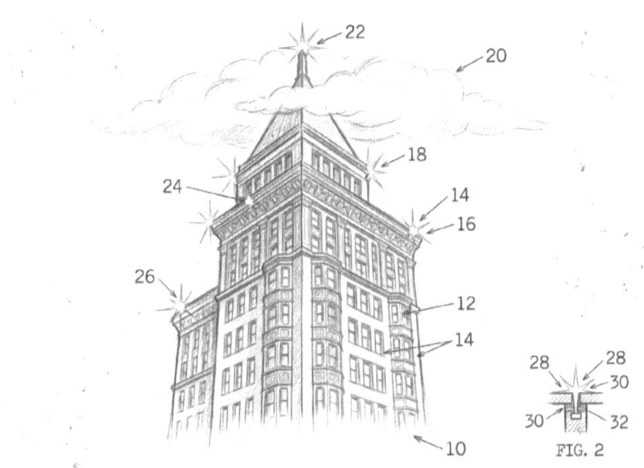

The High-Rise Hustle

Look, we really stared at the clouds and decided we needed to put a cubicle right in the middle of them. Europe is out here flexing with old dusty rocks, but we got ambition and a mountain of steel. We're basically trying to knock on God's door just to see if He's actually home. It's the ultimate high-altitude flex.

LIBERTY FACT

In December, 1903, The Wright brothers' first flight lasted only twelve seconds, but the day ended when a sudden gust of wind caught the Flyer and rolled it across the sand, wrecking the frame beyond repair. It was history's first recorded instance of nature's "return to sender" policy.

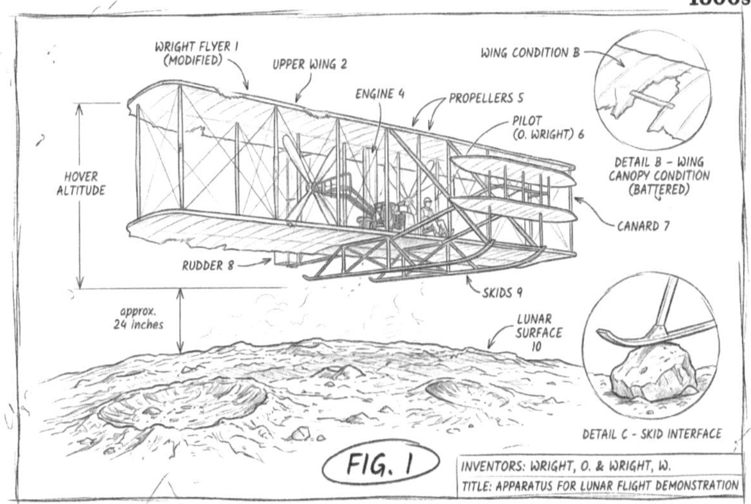

The Wright Stuff

Two bike mechanics from Ohio decided gravity was optional and flew a powered wooden glider over cow pastures and sand dunes. We went from flying 120 feet to parking a literal car on the moon in sixty-six years. That's the American vibe—give us 120 feet, and we're taking it all the way to the stars, man.

LIBERTY FACT

In 1914, Ford debuted the $5-a-day wage, doubling pay to ensure his workers could actually buy the cars they built. It was a masterstroke of economic liberty that turned laborers into consumers. After all, it's hard to sell the "American Dream" to a guy who's too broke to drive it.

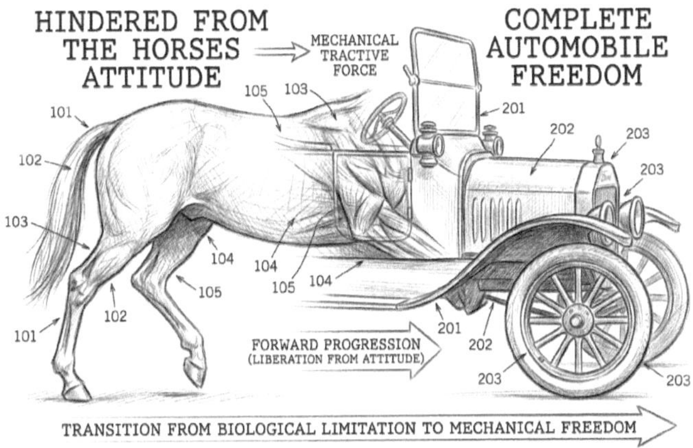

Model T: The Great Escape

Henry Ford saw that horse had a mind of its own and said, "Nah, brother, we need a machine that doesn't argue."

He put those cars on a line so we could finally ditch the horse's attitude and find real liberty. If that Model T could climb it, you owned it. It wasn't just a car; it was a "get out of the stable free" card. We finally had a way to outrun our problems at twenty miles per hour.

LIBERTY FACT

The U.S. finished the Panama Canal in 1914. We moved 240 million cubic yards of earth and rock. It cost $375 million. It was an engineering miracle that basically made the world 7,800 miles smaller.

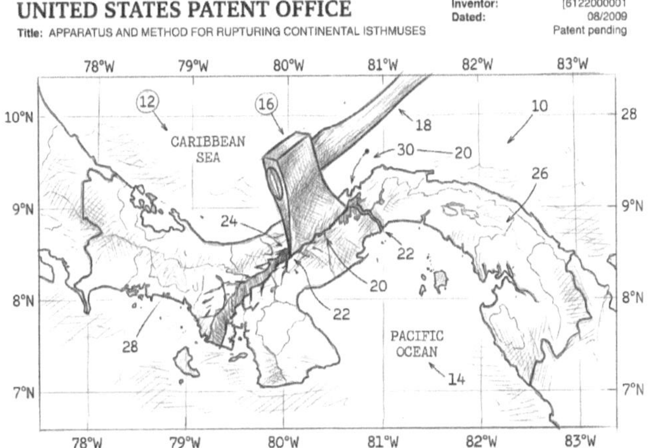

The World's Shortest Shortcut

We stared at South America and we simply determined, "That's too much ocean." So we just deleted a chunk of Panama. We dug through a whole jungle because we're just not 'three-week-detour' people. We will literally move a mountain just to save twenty minutes on shipping a toaster.

LIBERTY FACT

The 18th Amendment (Prohibition) was passed in 1920. It was a massive failure and led to the rise of organized crime. We realized our mistake 13 years later and passed the 21st Amendment in 1933 to repeal it. We're the only country to pass a Constitutional Amendment just to say, "Yeah, my bad. Let's try that again."

Jazz and Juice in the Shadows

Man, we really tried to ban a whole liquid! We're the same people that'll start a riot if you touch our thermostat, and we thought we could just cancel gin? All we did was make the party illegal and the jazz louder. We basically turned "minding your business with a glass" into a high-stakes heist.

LIBERTY FACT

Gutzon Borglum started carving Mt. Rushmore in 1927. The project cost $989,992. Over 400 workers used dynamite to remove 90% of the stone. It's a miracle nobody blew up their own mustache.

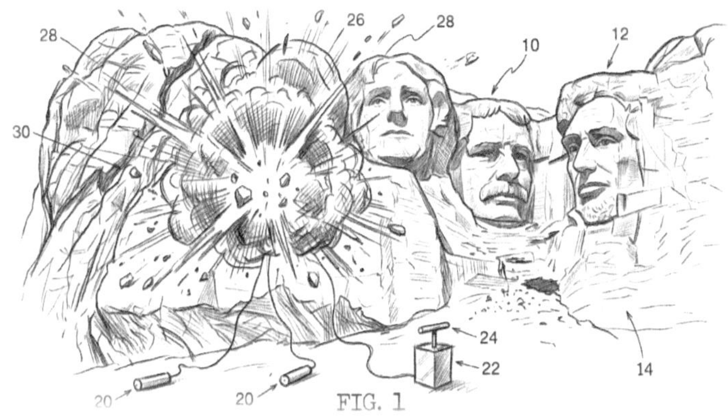

Mountain Makeovers

Man, we saw this perfectly good mountain in South Dakota and just thought, "This thing needs some faces on it, brother." So we blew it up for fourteen years until we got four giant dudes just staring into space. It's like the ultimate yard art, but with more dynamite and way less permit. Just some big, rocky brothers watching the sunset forever.

LIBERTY FACT

The Cold War generally lasted from the end of WWII in 1945 until the collapse of the Soviet Union in 1991. We spent the whole time waiting for something that didn't happen, but we got the Internet, microwave ovens, and a man on the moon out of the deal, so... win?

The Neighborhood Watch

What is the deal with the Cold War? We built these massive missiles just to show the world that liberty has the biggest yard on the block. It's the ultimate flex! We spent forty years proving our American grill is way better than whatever they're cooking over there. We weren't just defending a border; we were making sure the whole neighborhood stayed free.

LIBERTYFACT

The first "All You Can Eat" buffet was started in Las Vegas in 1946. It was called "The Buckaroo Buffet" and cost $1. It's the most successful experiment in human willpower ever conducted. We love a budget-friendly victory.

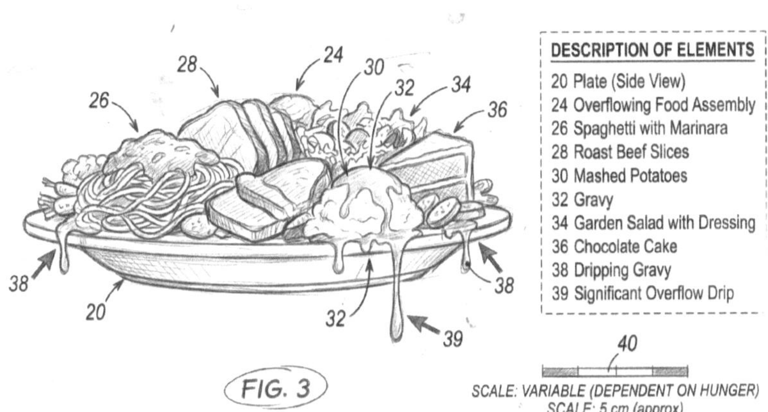

FIG. 3

The Bill of Bites

Bruh, only in America do we invent a "buffet" and treat it like an Olympic sport! We're the only people who think "winning" means sitting in the parking lot for an hour just to catch our breath. We don't ask "why?"; we ask, "Can you deep-fry that freedom and add some bacon?" It's not about hunger; it's about dominance.

LIBERTY FACT

The first microwave oven (the "Radarange") was sold in 1947. It was 6 feet tall and cost $5,000. That's a lot of money just to make a potato slightly faster. Now you can buy one for $40 that has a setting specifically for popcorn.

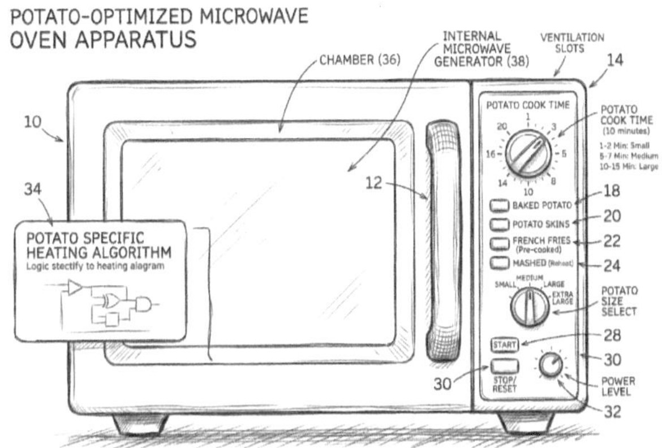

The Warp-Speed Republic

We harnessed the literal power of stars just so a potato wouldn't take all afternoon. That's the American spirit—we don't wait for the future; we build it by lunch. We'll drop a bag of cash to snatch back sixty seconds because our time is too precious to waste. We turned the clock into a race and started sprinting before the bell even rang.

LIBERTY FACT

In the 1950s, a new technology called the "7-inch 45 rpm single" record made it possible for kids to buy their own songs for the first time. It started the whole "youth culture" that still has us arguing about whether the 90s were better than the 80s.

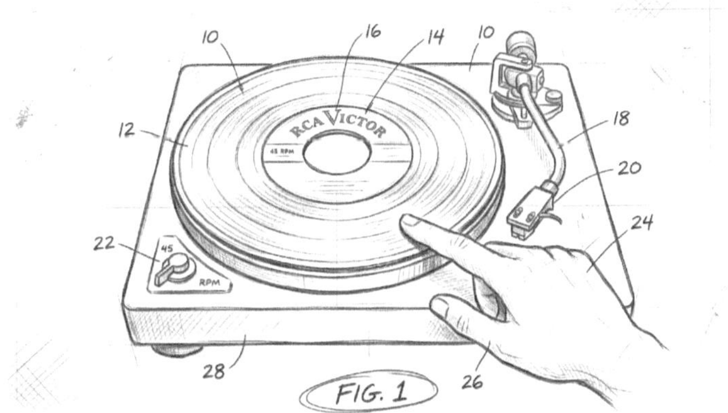

The Star-Spangled Spinner

RCA Victor basically gave America the greatest gift ever—tiny records that don't break when you drop them. We invented these plastic spiders so we could blast rock and roll at maximum volume. It's a free country, so you can buy like, fifty of them. Heck yes, American engineering is flippin' sweet.

LIBERTY FACT

The first fully enclosed indoor shopping mall opened in Minnesota in 1956. They built it indoors because it was in Minnesota. If it were in Hawaii, it would just be called "outside."

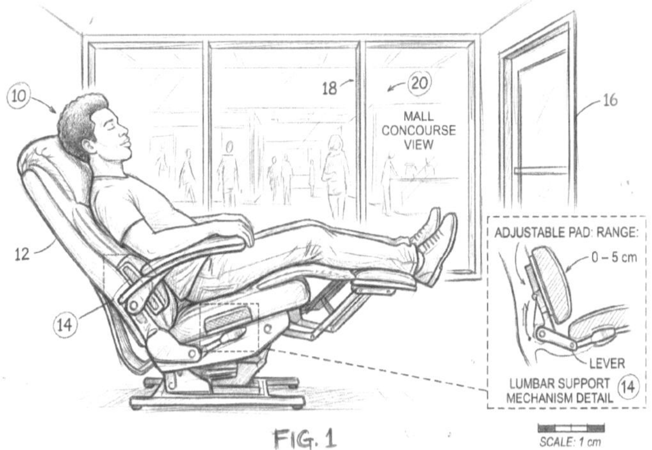

The Climate-Controlled Colony

We looked at the outdoors and said, "It's too cold brother. Let's build a giant box, put a fountain and an Orange Julius in the middle, and call it 'culture.'" The mall was our national town square for forty years. It was a place where teenagers could get lost and fathers could fall asleep in a "lumbar support" recliner at the department store.

LIBERTY FACT

President Eisenhower signed the Federal-Aid Highway Act in 1956. He wanted the Interstates so the military could move quickly across the country in case of a Cold War emergency. Now, we use them to move quickly to a different time zone for a three-day weekend.

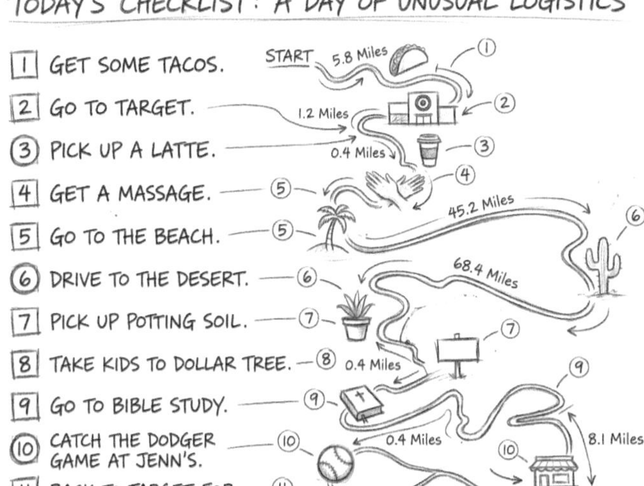

Sweet Infrastructure Gains

We built like, 48,000 miles of highway just so I can floor it at 85 while eating a taco. It's the most incredible feat ever, and we just use it to get to Target for some sweet deals. We achieved maximum efficiency basically just for maximum convenience. It's pretty much the best thing ever built.

LIBERTY FACT

Apollo 11 landed on the Moon on July 20, 1969. The "computer" that navigated it had less processing power than a modern musical greeting card. They were basically flying with a calculator and hopes. That's that American ingenuity power.

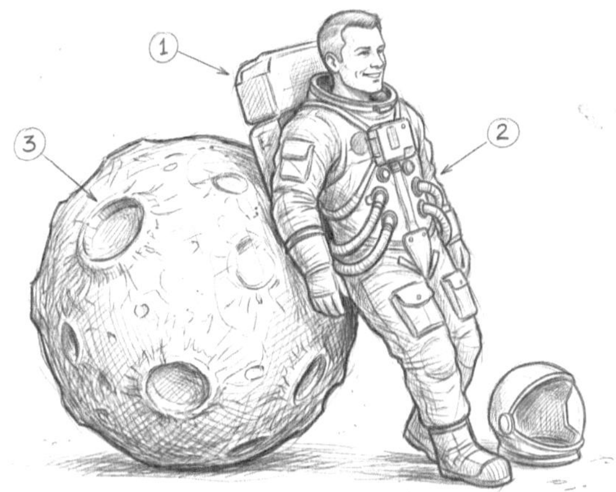

FIG. 1

Houston, the Neighbors are Jealous

We went to the moon specifically to look the world in the eye and say, "Yeah, we're here." We didn't even have a plan! It's like buying the most expensive, chrome-plated grill just so the neighbors have to smell your greatness. We literally flew 238,000 miles just for the ultimate cosmic bragging rights. It was a total power move.

1776-2026

How to Freedom
Without Hurting Yourself

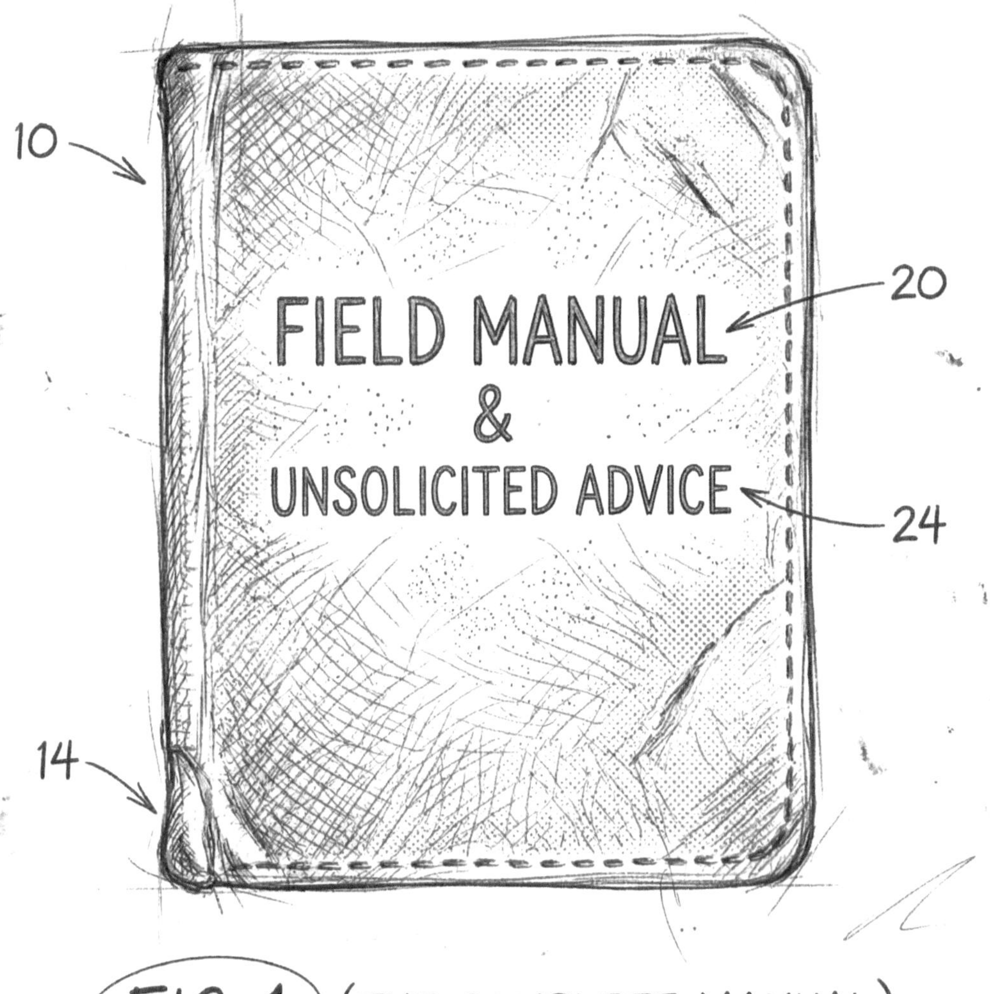

FIG. 1 (THE COMPLETE MANUAL)

The Proper Way to Inspect a Historical Marker

A HISTORICAL MARKER IS THE ULTIMATE TACTICAL RETREAT. WHEN THE KIDS START MELTING DOWN AND THE WIFE WANTS TO KNOW WHERE THE CAR IS PARKED, YOU SIMPLY LOCK YOUR KNEES, STROKE YOUR CHIN, AND ENGAGE THE "HEAVY THINKING" STARE. YOU AREN'T ACTUALLY READING—YOU'RE PERFORMING FOR THE PARK RANGERS AND THE BYSTANDERS, PROVING YOU AREN'T JUST SOME UNCULTURED TOURIST. AFTER TEN SECONDS OF COMMUNING WITH THE GHOSTS OF 1776, YOU PAT THE PLAQUE, MUTTER, "WHAT A TIME TO BE ALIVE," AND FINALLY EARN THE LEGAL RIGHT TO TOSS YOUR TAFFY WRAPPER IN THE NEARBY BIN. STAY PROFESSIONAL.

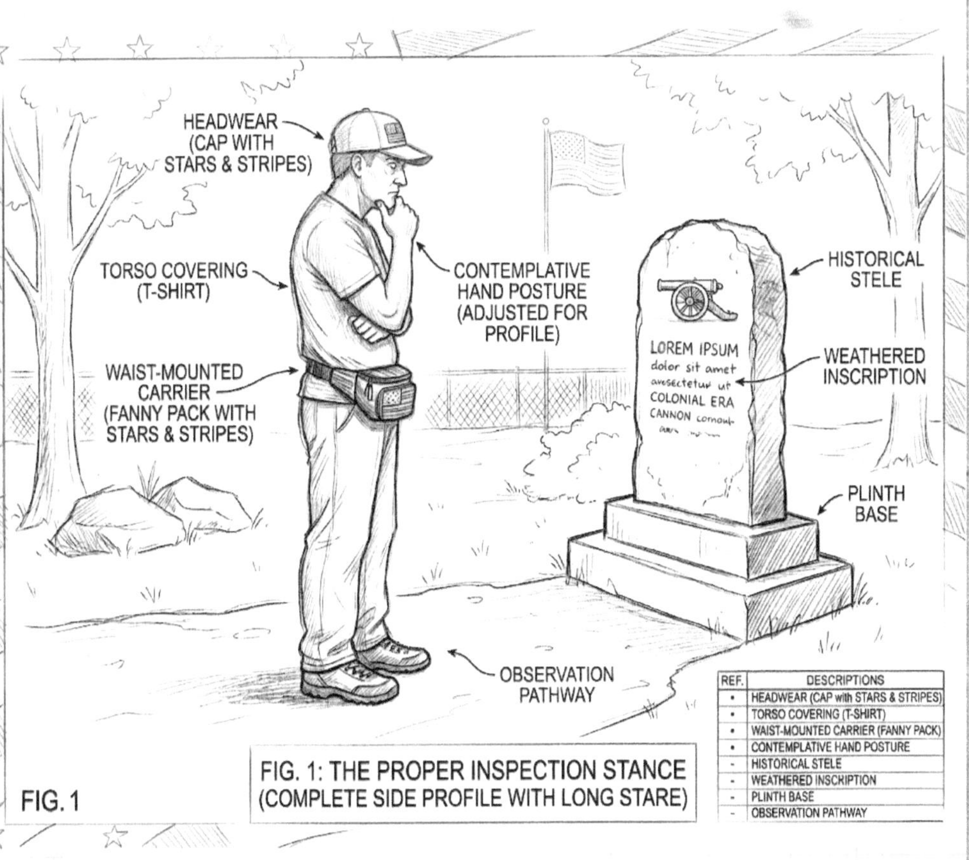

FIG. 1: THE PROPER INSPECTION STANCE (COMPLETE SIDE PROFILE WITH LONG STARE)

FIG. 1

REF.	DESCRIPTIONS
•	HEADWEAR (CAP with STARS & STRIPES)
•	TORSO COVERING (T-SHIRT)
•	WAIST-MOUNTED CARRIER (FANNY PACK)
•	CONTEMPLATIVE HAND POSTURE
-	HISTORICAL STELE
-	WEATHERED INSCRIPTION
-	PLINTH BASE
-	OBSERVATION PATHWAY

Lost Art #2

The How-To:
Navigation of the 4th of July BBQ.

THE SAFE ZONE: LOCATED EXCLUSIVELY NEAR THE COOLER FILLED WITH THE COLD ROOT BEER. THIS IS WHERE YOU CAN DISCUSS THE WEATHER, STANDARD LAWN METRICS, AND HOW HARD IT IS TO GET A USB PLUG IN ON THE FIRST TRY.

THE DANGER ZONE: LOCATED AT THE BUFFET TABLE, FOCUSING ON THE POTATO SALAD. IF THAT BOWL IS SITTING IN DIRECT SUNLIGHT AT 1:00 PM AND THE LID ISN'T CONDENSATION-FREE, YOU MUST AVOID IT AT ALL COSTS. THAT SALAD IS CURRENTLY A BIOLOGICAL WEAPON.

THE "BURGER STANDOFF": THE BBQ GRILL ZONE RIGHT NEXT TO THE GRILL. NEVER ASK THE GRILLER IF THE BURGERS ARE DONE. YOU CAN ONLY OFFER NON-VERBAL, "NODDING-OF-APPROVAL" LOGIC. LET HIM DO HIS WORK.

THE "CIVIL WAR CORNER": THE BACK-LEFT CORNER OF THE YARD. UNCLE MIKE IS THERE. DO NOT MAKE EYE CONTACT. IF YOU GO NEAR THIS ZONE, HE WILL EXPLAIN BAYONET LOGISTICS TO YOU FOR TWO CONSECUTIVE HOURS AND YOU WON'T BE ABLE TO ESCAPE UNTIL THE FIREWORKS START.

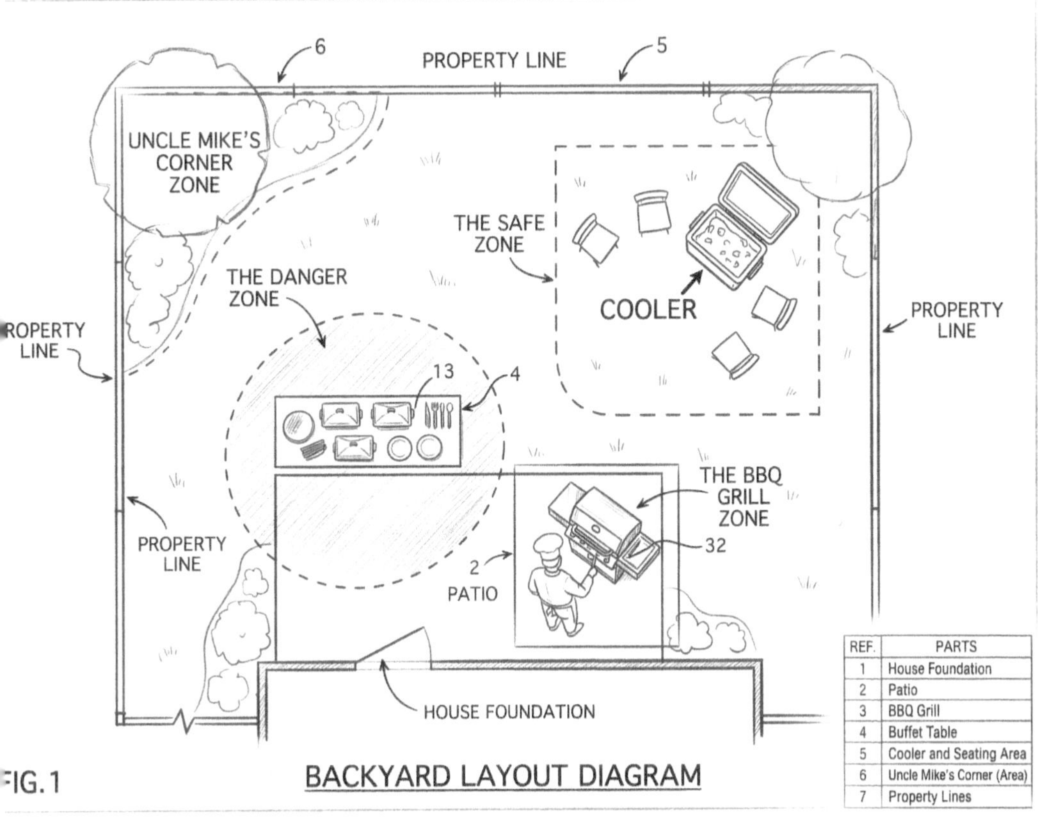

BACKYARD LAYOUT DIAGRAM

FIG. 1

REF.	PARTS
1	House Foundation
2	Patio
3	BBQ Grill
4	Buffet Table
5	Cooler and Seating Area
6	Uncle Mike's Corner (Area)
7	Property Lines

Understanding the Structural Engineering of the Independence Day Plate

LOAD BEARING BRISKET: THE HEAVY PROTEIN ANCHOR PLACED PRECISELY IN THE CENTER FOR STRUCTURAL BALANCE.

THE POTATO SALAD RETAINING WALL: A STARCHY, STRUCTURAL DAM BUILT TO PROTECT THE HOT DOG BUN FROM MOISTURE.

THE BAKED BEAN LIQUEFACTION ZONE: THE HIGH-RISK AREA WHERE SAUCE THREATENS TO BREACH THE CARDBOARD BARRIER.

CRITICAL FAILURE POINT: THE THUMB-GRIP EDGE THAT BENDS DANGEROUSLY UNDER THE WEIGHT OF FREEDOM.

BACKYARD LOGIC:
WE HOLD THESE TRUTHS TO BE SELF-EVIDENT: ALWAYS DOUBLE-PLATE.

STRUCTURAL INTEGRITY ANALYSIS OF THE PAPER PLATE BBQ-LOAD CROSS-SECTION (FIG. 1)

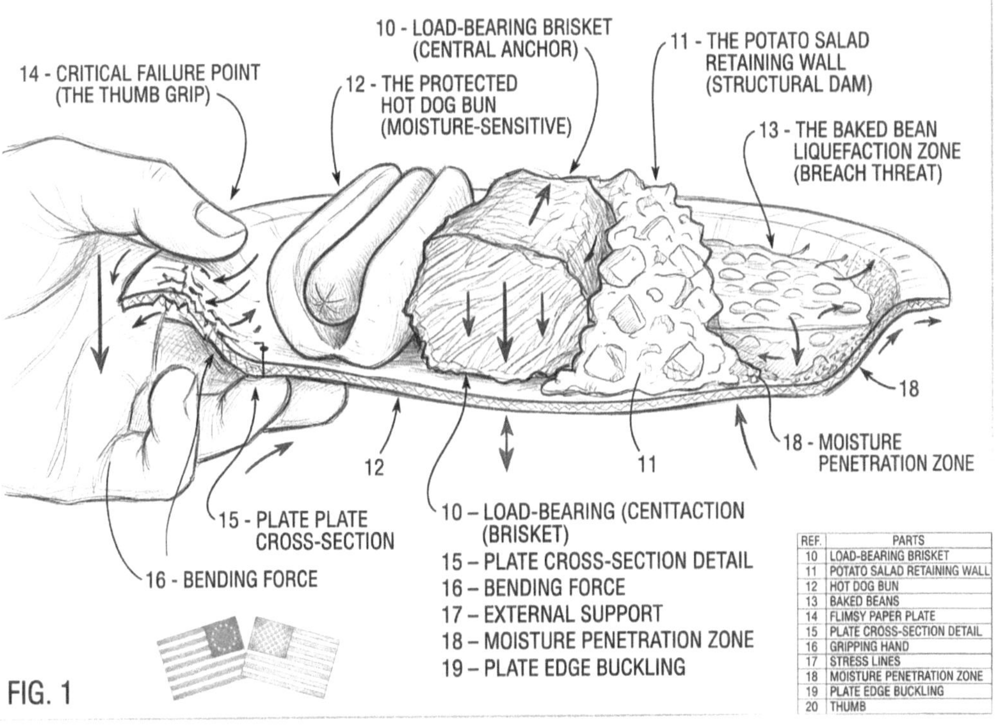

REF.	PARTS
10	LOAD-BEARING BRISKET
11	POTATO SALAD RETAINING WALL
12	HOT DOG BUN
13	BAKED BEANS
14	FLIMSY PAPER PLATE
15	PLATE CROSS-SECTION DETAIL
16	GRIPPING HAND
17	STRESS LINES
18	MOISTURE PENETRATION ZONE
19	PLATE EDGE BUCKLING
20	THUMB

FIG. 1

Operation "Suburban Shockwave": Where to retreat with your family at the 4th of July Driveway Perimeter

THE LAUNCH PAD: THE EXACT END OF THE DRIVEWAY WHERE DAD STANDS WITH A LONG-BARREL BBQ LIGHTER.

THE HASTY RETREAT VECTOR: A DOTTED LINE SHOWING THE PRECISE SPRINT PATH FROM THE IGNITED MORTAR TUBE BACK TO THE LAWN CHAIRS.

UNPREDICTABLE TRAJECTORY ZONE: THE BLAST RADIUS OF THE DISCOUNT "SCREAMING MIMI" THAT TIPPED OVER.

CIVILIAN BUNKER: THE DESIGNATED SAFE VIEWING AREA LOCATED BEHIND THE FAMILY MINIVAN.

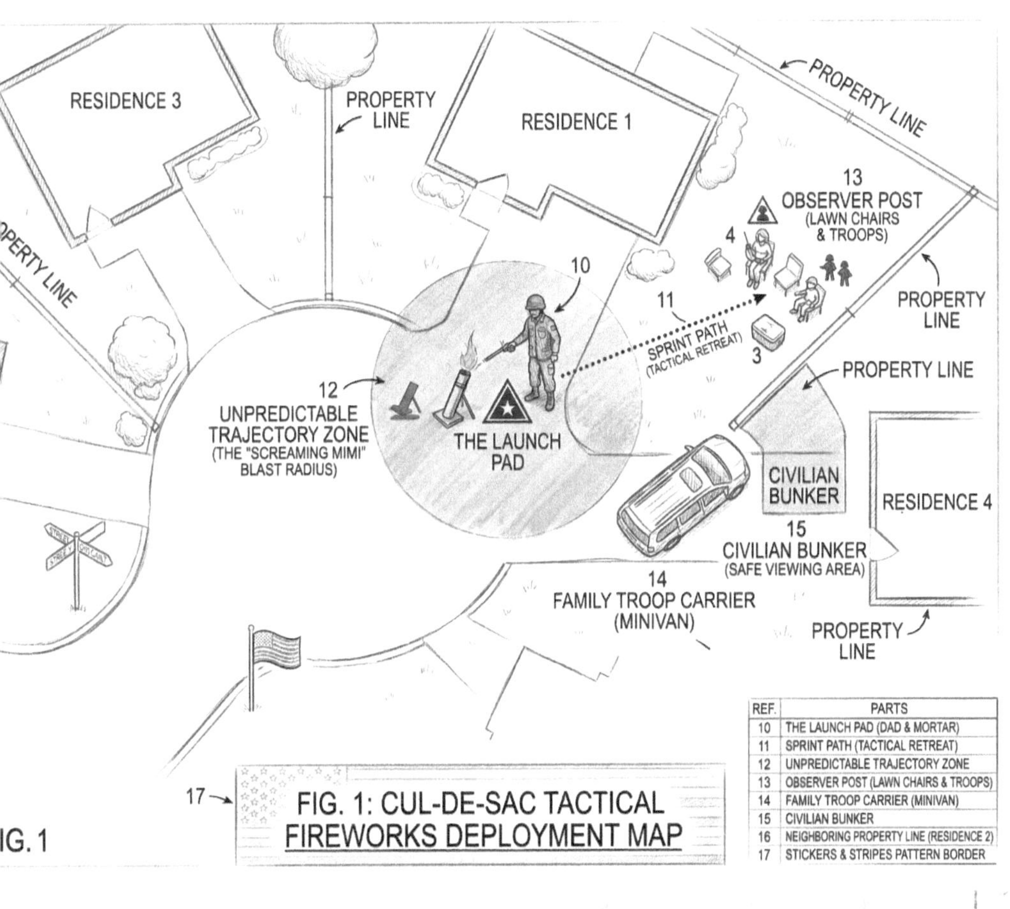

REF.	PARTS
10	THE LAUNCH PAD (DAD & MORTAR)
11	SPRINT PATH (TACTICAL RETREAT)
12	UNPREDICTABLE TRAJECTORY ZONE
13	OBSERVER POST (LAWN CHAIRS & TROOPS)
14	FAMILY TROOP CARRIER (MINIVAN)
15	CIVILIAN BUNKER
16	NEIGHBORING PROPERTY LINE (RESIDENCE 2)
17	STICKERS & STRIPES PATTERN BORDER

FIG. 1: CUL-DE-SAC TACTICAL FIREWORKS DEPLOYMENT MAP

FIG. 1

Phase Three:
The Modern Marvels

(The Home Stretch)

1900s - 2026

**From horse-power to rocket-power and pixels.
The ultimate upgrade.**

The term "Semiquincentennial" is a real word, but it's so hard to say that most people just call it "The 250th." It comes from semi (half), quin (five), and centennial (100). "It's a lot of syllables for a birthday party."

Eagle-Grease and Varsity Dreams

We're two-fifty deep, just a wild fella in a denim vest trying to outrun a tornado. We're shouting over the fence at Canada while wearing our 1776 jersey like we still got that varsity glow. It's that constant startup energy— just pure eagle-grease and high-octane liberty.

GPS (Global Positioning System) was originally a Department of Defense project started in the 1970s. It wasn't fully opened for high-quality civilian use until 2000. Before that, we had to rely on "The Map That You Can Never Fold Back Correctly."

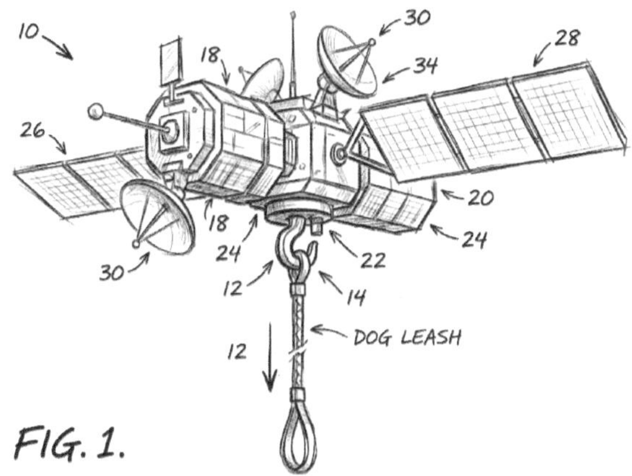

FIG. 1.

The Celestial Dog Leash

We've outsourced our sanity to a robot three miles up. I'm standing in my living room, but if my phone says I'm in a Taco Bell parking lot, I'm ordering a burrito. We don't believe we exist until a satellite pings our location. It's a space leash—we're just lost souls waiting for the blue dot to catch up.

*The Pet Rock was a massive fad in 1975. For $3.95,
you bought a regular rock that came with a cardboard
"pet carrier" and a manual on how to "train" it.
It made the inventor a millionaire in six months.
That's the American dream, man.*

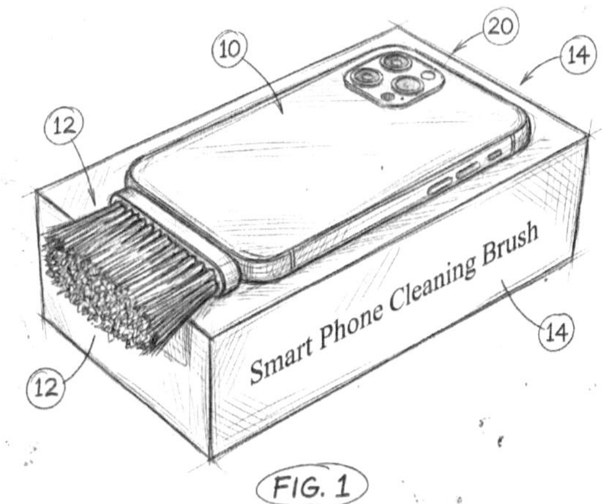

Selling the Unnecessary

We have a talent for turning useless ideas into multi-million dollar industries. We'll buy a blanket with sleeves, spray-on hair, or even a literal rock in a box just to see if it works. America is the only place where "it doesn't exist" is just a marketing challenge we haven't conquered yet.

Americans consume about 50 billion burgers a year. If you stacked them up, they'd reach the moon and back... about 32 times. We aren't just eating; we're building a caloric ladder to the stars.

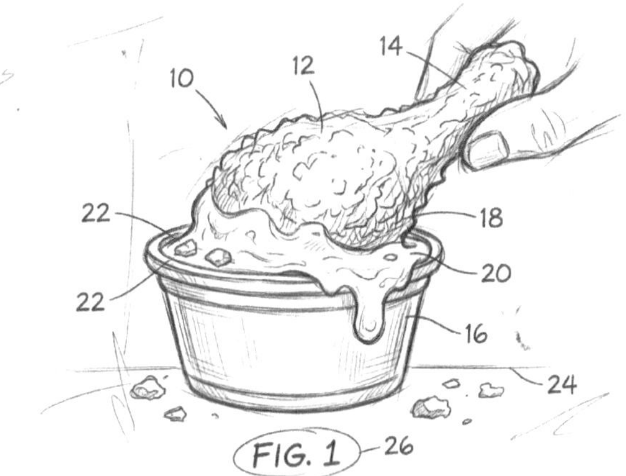

The "Double Down" Courage

We are the only nation that looked at two pieces of fried chicken and said, "What if these were the bread?"
We invented the KFC Double Down because we decided that carbohydrates were the enemy, but sodium was our best friend. It's that "Why Not?" energy. We don't ask if we should; we just want to know if it comes with a side of ranch.

LIBERTY FACT

NASA's Space Shuttle program, active from 1981 to 2011, pioneered the world's first reusable spacecraft, deploying satellites and building the ISS. It was a masterpiece of Cold War engineering—a high-tech marvel that proved we could conquer the stars and still land with the grace of a falling brick.

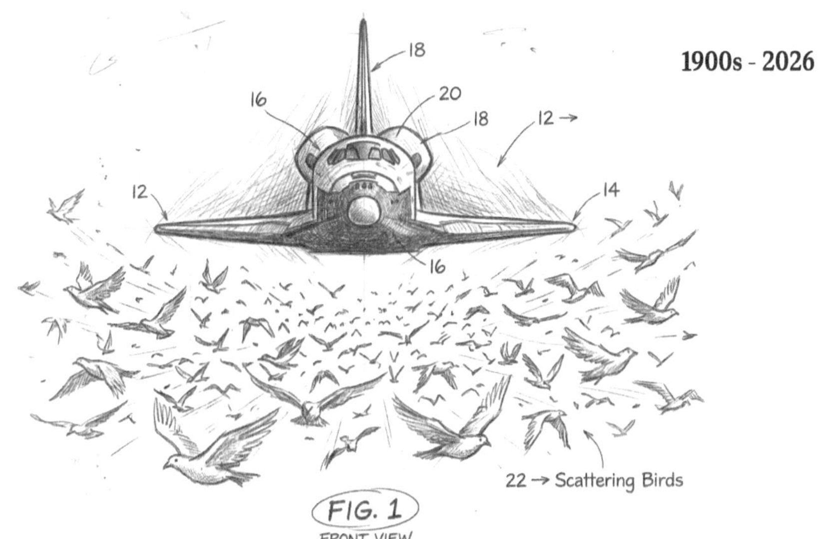

The Cosmic Cargo Van

We built a massive, high-tech space truck just to show the universe how it's done, then decided we didn't even need engines for the landing. That's pure American confidence—launching on a pillar of fire and coming home on a wing and a prayer. It's the world's most expensive, patriotic game of lawn darts.

LIBERTY FACT

In preparation for the millennium year, Y2K, the U.S. government spent over $100 billion to ensure national stability, only for the most notable "glitch" to be a Delaware bus pass machine failing. We spent billions to protect the grid, but the machines just wanted a day off.

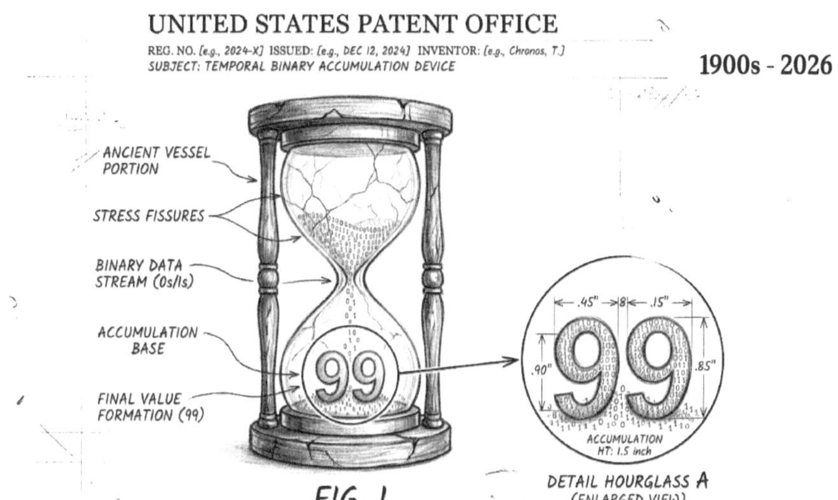

Y2K: Almost Folding for a Typo

We built the most advanced networks in history, then spent a whole year terrified that "00" would make the world implode and we'd all stop breathing. After everything we've survived, did we really think a calendar glitch was the end? We didn't stray from our roots; we're Americans. We don't fold—we just upgrade. That's that undefeated patriotic spirit, brother.

In 2026, it is estimated that over 160 billion packages are shipped globally. A huge percentage of those are just Americans ordering "bulk replacement socks" at 2:00 AM because we don't want to do laundry.

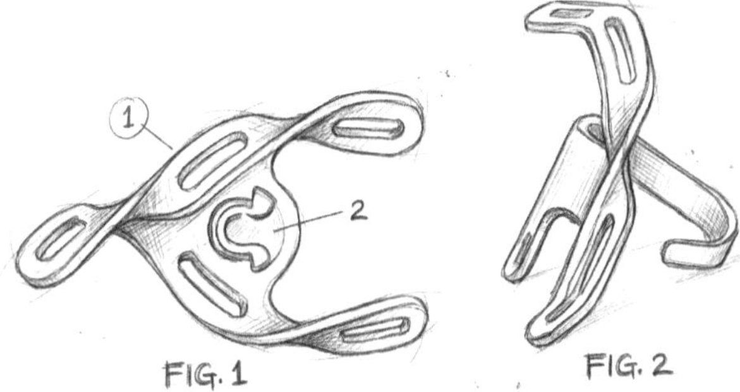

Museum of Maybe Useful

My garage isn't storage—it's a retirement plan for objects with no current purpose. I've got wood scraps that look like they lost a fight, boxes for things I don't own anymore, and a collection of screws that feel emotionally significant. There's also that one metal thing—no idea what it is, but I'd defend it in court. My wife calls it junk. I call it the American dream with dust on it.

The Internet (ARPANET) began in 1969 as a way for four university computers to talk to each other. Now, it's a global network used primarily to watch videos of people falling off trampolines and to let our refrigerators tell us we're out of milk.

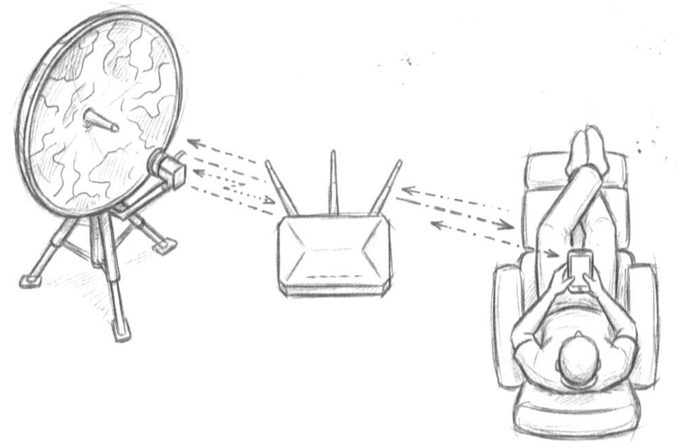

The Renegade Router

We took a global military communications grid and turned it into a 24/7 buffet of memes and lawnmower racing. That's the American dream: taking a trillion dollars of fiber optics meant for secrets and using it to find out which type of cheese matches our personality. If it's got a signal, we're gonna find a way to use it for something completely unintended. It's high-speed liberty, baby!

The first TV commercial aired in 1941. It was for Bulova watches, lasted 10 seconds, and cost $9. Today, a 30-second Super Bowl ad costs over $7 million, and half the time, we don't even know what they're selling until the very end.

FIG. 1

Freedom, Now Streaming Monthly

We've got a thousand channels, six apps, and somehow I'm still scrolling like I'm searching for lost history. Every show costs extra, every menu feels like paperwork, and after all that effort, somehow we end up on a rerun like it's a national compromise. Makes a person miss the simpler days of 1776, when at least the options were clear.

There is actually a "secret" vaulted room behind the heads on Mt. Rushmore. It was intended to hold the nation's most important documents. It doesn't have a map to a hoard of Templar gold, but it does have a record of why the mountain was carved.

The National Scavenger Hunt

What is the deal with the news? We treat the news like a game of Clue. We don't want the facts; we want the scavenger hunt! We're convinced there's a secret map behind every bill. It's that "what's really goin' on" energy that keeps us addicted. We aren't looking for answers; we're just chasing that national treasure high, brother.

LIBERTY FACT

During the Bicentennial (1976), the U.S. was so excited that we painted fire hydrants like revolutionary soldiers and released a special red-white-and-blue quarter. In 2026, we've gone even bigger, with drones replacing fireworks in cities that are "too dry" for actual explosions.

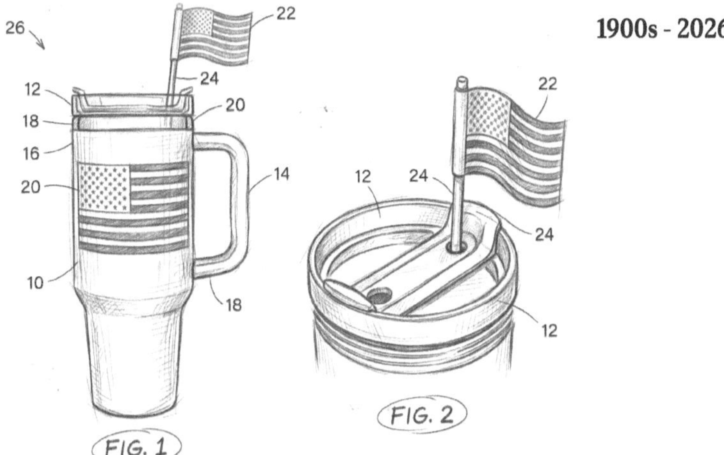

Ice-Cold Independence

It's 2026, and I just bought a $60 insulated tumbler because the box said "Declaration of Hydration." It's basically a steel bucket with a flag on it, but I felt like if I didn't buy it, the British might come back. Now I'm drinking lukewarm coffee out of a cup that has more rights than I do. We're the masters of the branded hustle, man—if it's shiny and says "Limited Edition Liberty," I'm in.

American movies and music account for a massive portion of the world's entertainment. Hollywood produces over 600 films a year. We are essentially a giant story-telling machine that happens to have a very large navy.

The Global Uniform

You can hike into a remote desert and find a guy in a Yankees hat drinking a Coke. We don't just export products; we export the "vibe." We're the world's leading producer of stuff you only bought because a movie hero looked cool. That's not a hat; it's American swagger!

LIBERTY FACT

In 2015, SpaceX successfully landed a Falcon 9 rocket booster vertically, ending the era of "disposable" space travel. By proving rockets could be reused, the cost of liberty among the stars plummeted. It's a giant leap for mankind—and a huge win for anyone who hates throwing away the car after one road trip.

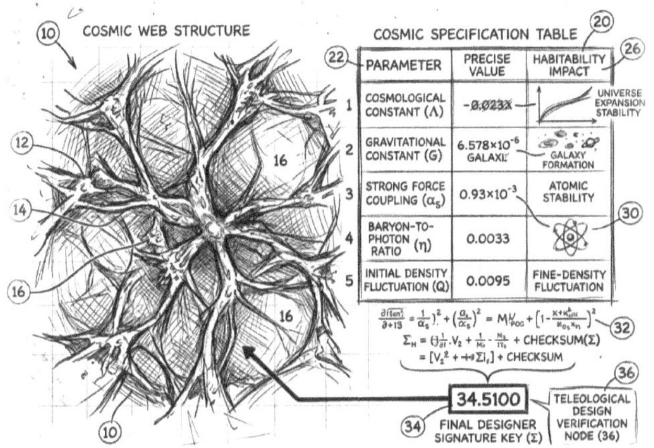

PARAMETER	PRECISE VALUE	HABITABILITY IMPACT
COSMOLOGICAL CONSTANT (Λ)	-0.0233%	UNIVERSE EXPANSION STABILITY
GRAVITATIONAL CONSTANT (G)	6.578×10^{-6} GALAXIES	GALAXY FORMATION
STRONG FORCE COUPLING (α_s)	0.93×10^{-3}	ATOMIC STABILITY
BARYON-TO-PHOTON RATIO (η)	0.0033	
INITIAL DENSITY FLUCTUATION (Q)	0.0095	FINE-DENSITY FLUCTUATION

Peeking at the Source Code

We sent a million-mile golden selfie stick into the void just
to prove that even the edge of time is American territory.
Hubble gave us blurry "maybe" vibes, but Webb showed
up in ultra-HD. Turns out the universe isn't a messy glitch;
we just finally upgraded our eyes to see the Creator's been
running the whole show in IMAX. It's not just space;
it's a high-definition flex from the Heavens!

In the 1960s, New Jersey researchers accidentally discovered Cosmic Microwave Background radiation—the "echo" of the universe's creation—while trying to fix a noisy antenna. It's a foundational pillar of modern science, proving that Americans can't even try to tune a radio without accidentally stumbling upon a ground breaking scientific discovery.

The 250,000-Mile Epiphany

Artemis II rockets allowed humans to travel further than any in history, only for the crew to return gushing at the Creator's handiwork back home. It's the quintessential American spirit: we are so obsessed with "what's next" that we had to launch ourselves into a freezing, lifeless vacuum just to notice the paradise we were currently standing on.

In 1976 (the Bicentennial), we put a time capsule in the ground that won't be opened until 2076 (the Tricentennial). We are currently exactly at the halfway point. We are the "Middle Children" of history. We are currently "holding the root beer" while the next generation gets ready to do their own group project.

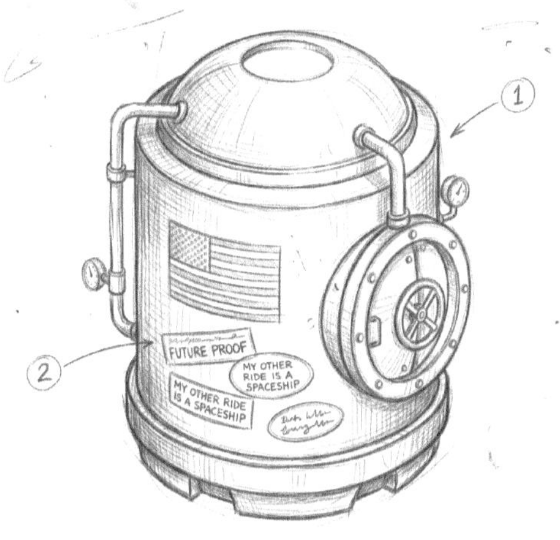

FIG. 1

The 500-Year Freedom Box

In 2026, we're burying a time capsule in Philly to show the year 2276 how we conquered the vibes. It's got a smartphone and a receipt for an $11 latte—proof that we lived the dream, one premium bean at a time. We're handing the future the keys to the American spirit and saying, "We did this in cargo shorts. Hold our root beer and see if you can top it!"

We love our Fourth of July fireworks, but most of the Founding Fathers didn't actually sign the Declaration until August 2, 1776. In that time, news moved slower than a line at the DMV. It took weeks for the colonies to even realize they were a country. We've always been great at celebrating—we just usually start the party before the paperwork is actually finished.

The Quarter-Millennium Flex

We've officially spent 250 years crushing the "figure it out" method of leadership. Sure, we're a loud, chaotic family, but look at the house we built! We're still the world's biggest experiment, and honestly, the momentum is electric. By year 300, we'll probably be hosting the Fourth of July on Mars, still proud, still messy, and still just getting started.

The Dad-Fact-Checker

"Back in my day..." facts to pass down

EX. **1.** <u>NO ONE ASKED FOR A 25% TIP JUST TO TAKE YOUR ORDER.</u>

2. _______________________

3. _______________________

4. _______________________

5. _______________________

6. _______________________

7. _______________________

8. _______________________

9. _______________________

10. _______________________

11. _______________________

12. _______________________

The Official Log of Unreasonable Charges

	Date	Modern Tea Taxes or Charges	Cost
EX.	2/15/26	AIRLINE BAGGAGE FEES	$50 PER BAG

US 2024/0000001 A1

DATE:

SIGNATURE:

SIGGNATURE:

PLAN A: Strategic BBQ Deployment

The "Ideal Conditions" schematic. Map out your primary grill coordinates, optimal cooler placement, and the "Safety Perimeter" for guests. Use this space to visualize & sketch the perfect Patriotic BBQ.

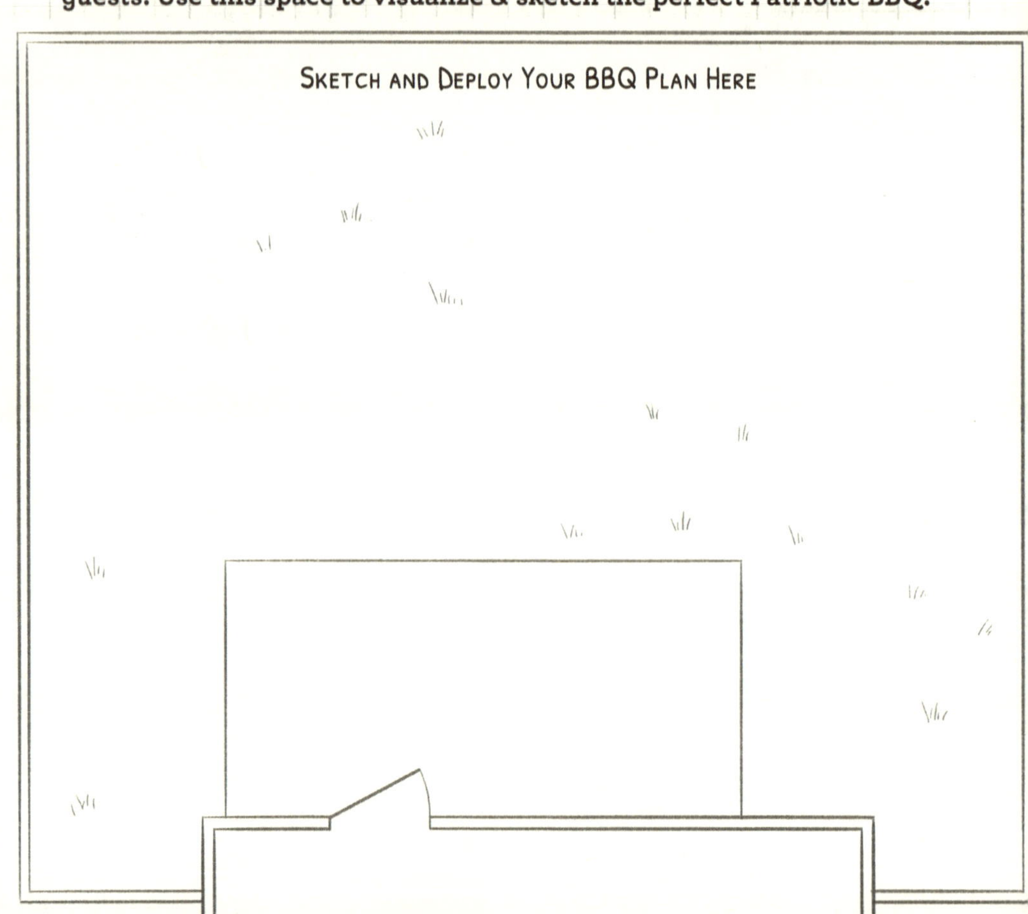

PLAN B: Emergency Contingency

For when the sky opens up or the propane runs dry. Sketch your
"head for the indoors" retreat extraction route. Failure to plan for a
"Kitchen" BBQ is a plan to eat soggy buns.

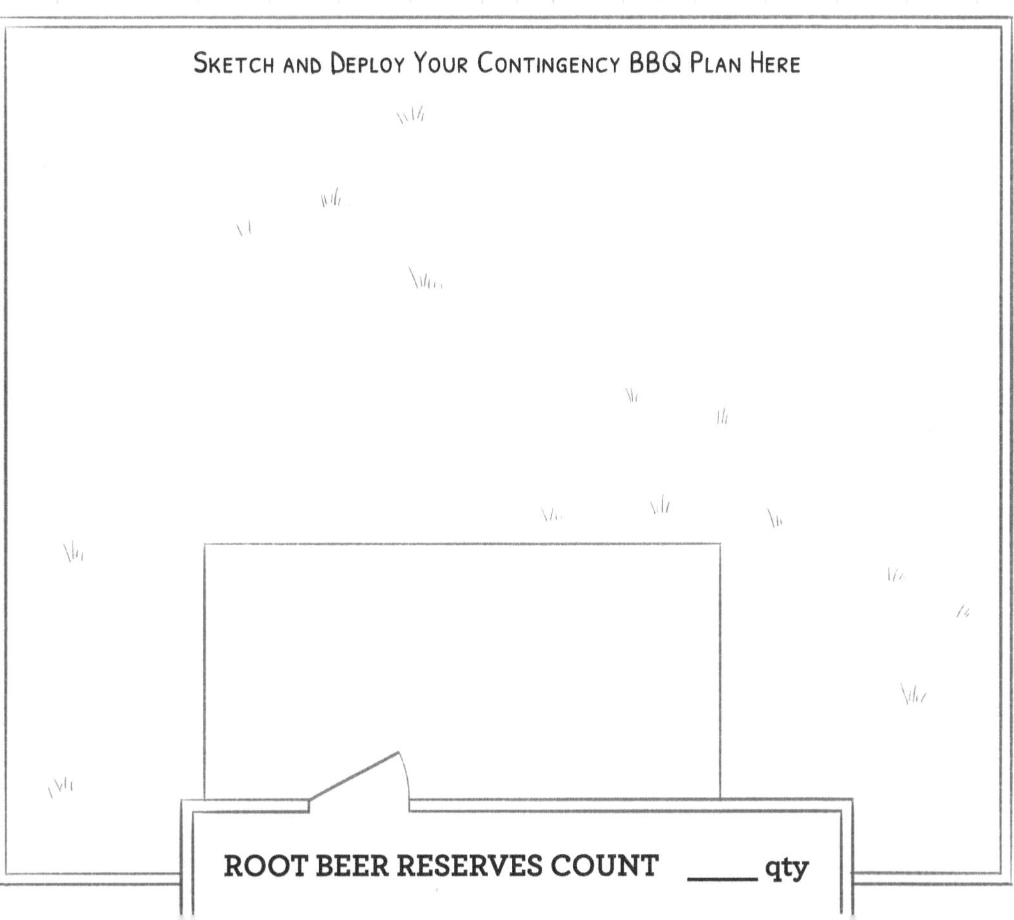

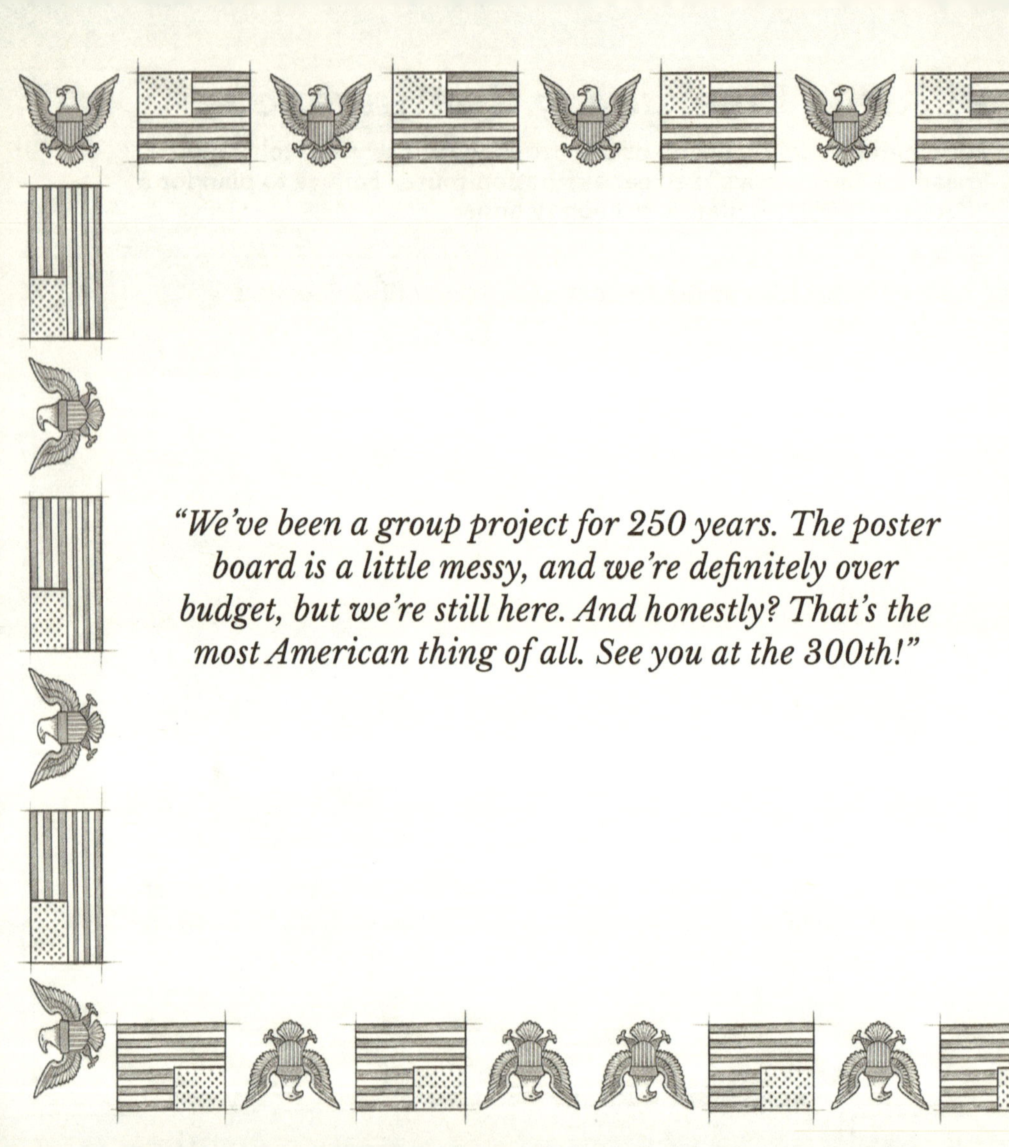

"We've been a group project for 250 years. The poster board is a little messy, and we're definitely over budget, but we're still here. And honestly? That's the most American thing of all. See you at the 300th!"

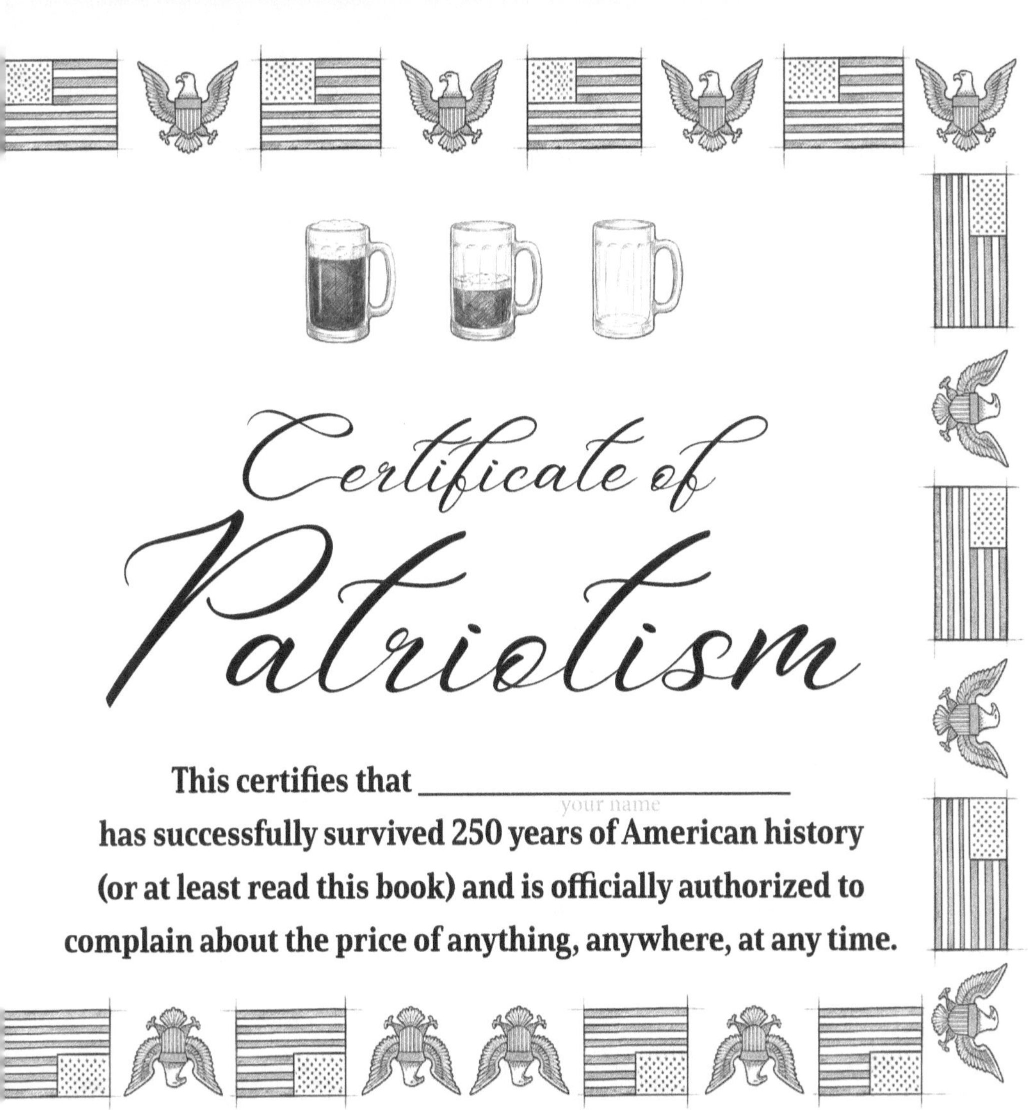

Certificate of Patriotism

This certifies that ______________________
your name
has successfully survived 250 years of American history
(or at least read this book) and is officially authorized to
complain about the price of anything, anywhere, at any time.

Backyard Logic

Backyard Logic is a group of people who believe most of the world's problems could be solved if everyone just sat on a porch for twenty minutes and minded their own business.

The Project Continues

- **PHASE 01** is just the beginning of the world's longest group project. Keep your white sneakers clean and your blueprints ready for the next two installments of *The Backyard Logic 250 Years Trilogy.*

- **PHASE 02:** *The Great American Side-Quest* (American Historical Facts/Unusual Stories) Expected June 2026

- **PHASE 03:** *The United States of "You Gotta See This"* ("Traveler's Guide" to the weirdest, most patriotic and beautiful parts of the USA) - Expected Summer 2026

If this book made you laugh even once, a short review helps more than you'd think.

@BACKYARDLOGICPRESS

UNITED STATES PATENT OFFICE

REG. NO. [e., 1777-1] ISSUED: [e.g. JULY 4, 1777] INVENTOR: [e.g. ROSS, B.]
SUBJECT: SYSTEM FOR A STAR CONFIGURATION (A NATIONAL ENSIGN COMPONENT)

— OVERALL CIRCLE DIAMETER